OBJECT PERMANENCE

OBJECT
PERMANENCE

Michelle Gil-Montero

ORNITHOPTER PRESS   PRINCETON

"Whatever you see, whatever can be taken away, is unspeakable."

—Alejandra Pizarnik

First Edition

Published by Ornithopter Press
www.ornithopterpress.com

ISBN 978-1-942723-07-3

Library of Congress Control Number: 2020932228

Art and Design by Mark Harris

CONTENTS

I

CREATION STORY ///////////////////////// 3
FIRST FORTY DAYS ///////////////////////// 4
SNAKES ///////////////////////////// 18
GIRL'S ROOM ///////////////////////// 19
SEQUENCE ///////////////////////////// 20
ONCE ///////////////////////////////// 25

II

SEASONS //////////////////////////////// 29
LACUNAE ///////////////////////////// 39

III

ATTACHED HOUSES ///////////////////// 51
COAST //////////////////////////////// 58
STRAY /////////////////////////////// 59
AIR AND DREAMS //////////////////////// 60
DIVINING ///////////////////////////// 70
FLOOD //////////////////////////////// 71
MY BOUNDARIES /////////////////////// 72
NOTATION //////////////////////////// 73

ACKNOWLEDGMENTS /////////////////// 75
ABOUT THE AUTHOR ///////////////// 77

I

"... in this, the
liminal
landscapes of the all-surrounding *isn't*."

—Gustaf Sobin

CREATION STORY

10/27/2018

Shadow. It fell, spatial. I mean, its distance pressed down. Crushed surface. Dark is the absence of light. Light is the absence of absence. Shadow twirls its cold mantle in space. Tell the child. Whose finger spins our loaded globe: day and night. Instead of talking about the darkness, always there, absent, show her about day and night. Shadow her about it. Say: This mist fills Pittsburgh. It learns us, the melancholy logic of bodies pulling through. Mist is the presence of absence. (Miss them, miss us.) This ceaseless mist.

FIRST FORTY DAYS

"It may be that, like the person who has touched death, the person who has experienced birth has been at the boundaries of life/non-life and therefore cannot directly re-enter the community."

—Tivka Frymer-Kensky

"I can't be myself / without first dying."

—Joseph Ceravolo

1

Muddled stillness
All summer

sun
punched the yellow jacket nest

Cavernous paper
valved like a parched heart

over and over
I let it

beat outside
my chest

2

Then rhythm
is my wandering
womb,

worldly
hum that no one
can explain.

August,
the nest

chews down
to a center room,

the hole in the middle.

3

In quarantine,
a humming
miasma of wasps rises
from the earth, and is beautiful,
like birth.

They fly into my trap, a bag of apple juice.
In the Suffocation of the Mother, 1603,
one becomes both the witch and the
bewitched.

I become

Lady Macbeth: bearded woman, apparition,
in her sleeping scene, with open eyes.

4

Inter-
locking

softness:

our edges

touch, smash
into shadow.

This poem—
like a bird shot

by an arrow
fletched with its own

feather—is a mother
poem.

5

Did I know

I was becoming
other?

Weary fluidity
of the blue

pen
signing consent

as one is wheeled
to sleep.

6

The glare
sears seeing—

Something moves out of the corner—
Often it is more   nothing

tumbling
from its silk sack.

I show you my
spider: a tattoo

in memory of the mythical
domesticity of

the mother—a profane
conflation of

legs entwined (the many
legs it takes to

float)
in memory

of the invention
of confessional art.

7

Focus on space:
The house.

Plain things
pained in relation.

The experience still
so still
it is invisible?

It will settle, I will tell you
where the edges belong.

8

I didn't want you to
remember—

ether

of my mother

on a soft

cloth—scrubbed

the sheets

for hours

leaning on the laundry sink

where blood

puddled in a fold.

9

I'm still laboring down

Playing dead in the river

How I pass the hours

Day after day

An egg separates in my fingers

There are sounds

I can't explain

The loneliness of calving ice

All night

I'll talk darkly to the trickle

That talks over me

10

Soft lip
of my vision

effacing

on

a rind of fruit

a nipple

late, silty light

bottoming
into thought

11

Small nostrils

intubated

dreg-heavy

bag of apple juice

Flashes hatch

in my head

then burrow out

carrying most of me

12

Lately, morning
sun behind veins

of blue
tumbling
spider leaf fists—

I sleep
in this light, soft,

twisted sheet,
thought—

vine I train
in my mind.

13

It ends
in the yard

where clouds shred
together.

Scum ram-
ifies
woodbine.

I water the rot.

It blossoms
into kisses

and the not-kisses
of wasps.

Needles
in the apples.

It is fall.

Last-year's party
glitter
in sparse grass.

SNAKES

Inverting wind, curtains wince—
Fine-nerved

linen, and in
the scoop-motion

          of a stitch
          a constellation of tense

pattern passes
into a single
hole.

Outside a boy

lights carbon snakes
which evolve together as one tear

catches another on a face.

GIRL'S ROOM

Reading to a daughter wondering

in how many languages is blue
an ooh and red a revving of
initial fervor

My old things are neither

hers nor mine
shelves of disconsolate
music boxes winding down

so the ballerina multiplies
inside her floor of mirrors

the steel comb tuned
to buckets full of cherry trees

The room almost moved
by its windless insistence

SEQUENCE

A sense of sequence   regenerates

a spine of sundress clasps

Evasive lines around the aging eye

                The light presents

a counterweight
to presence

             Perfunctory flight of crows

                (All excess flight

                   impacted in pose)

A boy streaks fireflies on his shirt

Stones jut in the sand

Mannequin's hipbones

A searchlight perfects the pause

in which a dark

divides its cloak

>   to bright-boned words
>   on the pubic frontis

They were chasing down places
                              chased down by strangeness

When the map short-circuited

Such is youth
                    The best defense is stillness

In half-tones

struggles out of clothes

                    Remembers her extremities

And catches herself

with the attitude of blessing

the bed that fades

into the cluttered floor

Unpicked stitches

the frenzied poise

of old trees—true,
the sex knuckled over

but the smell of hair

hung there

like a feathered lure

Mezzanined
by parentheses

her voice
trains its fingernails to curl

over the balcony

this coulisse of whispers
sewing so gracefully

insignias in the mind

ONCE

Once again begins
with once

then crunches underfoot
the always

unseasonable yellow
leaves

And restlessness
and once again

like charts accruing moons
at different degrees
of satiation

It is a time of many

half-thoughts
quick-edged as cut-outs

Once my window is a book
of esoteric recipes
for sleep

II

SEASONS

Spring's green-gone-
blue hills

shine immune
and in that light

desire is last
to scatter

Small white animals
are quicker

to feel and forget
a glance

with them, we live
a little less
present

End of fall
you are only solid

as a bird   and every verb
arbitrary

animates dead
leaves

that dance
its heat

of least
materials

No, alone is
toneless
tone

the new kitchen

lucid with
disuse

one, one, one, she
counts

or is it
none none, undone
erotically

ice
crushed
in the ice-textured
glass

The sign specifies *Live
Girls*

as flashes of debris
to see

on the side of the road
floral box

spring in
the dandelions.

Yellows
weedy ease

cheek-by-jowl
blooms of rip-gut
brome

I try
July and
all the shallow seeds burn

Hard-
lived water

in the harbor
you hold
still

so clouds move
over you

Where am I

in relation   I am pacing
myself

I can never read
Bataille while eating

or break an egg
cleanly in one hand

on sad days
anything reads
as an ethic

is the broken
egg less
naked

than the
shell

more innocent
than the hand

It snows
a filling meal
a thin line of pat sparrows

a fire
a failure to fit into that scent
murky pink of sweated sugar

what if you love something
you can only own
by arson

we are wakeful
it leaves
a grave circle
        in speech
a secret speed

voices age
husked, othered
equally by nudity
and cover

is it richer

the kiss   through
cloth however
confused

wet bag of fruit
last of the season

LACUNAE

early light
linted with
thought

mangle the
pulp

into paper

desirous-
white

sounds

violent water

highway's
embattled
quiet

hums
to brim

with the insufficiencies
of words

no
repetition is

never
emphasis

it
warms us

to warning

dull companion

stutters
to savor

the music of
words losing use

power
lines digress into moss

what I see
farther, bluer
with futurity

hills
filtered through a
closeness

they can't stand,
can't meet

so many things

are not

early light

refines

un-

being

the hills fade blue

and false—what I call hills

to mean a feeling-

followed, flowing

into roads

clouds

have voluptuous

names, nudge

nothing

a word

like a thing

afraid to touch

a thing, caress

the head of heather

hair

ash glittering, ready

to collapse

its

stillness
yes, but

as if
nervous

burnt toast
pumice stone

gravel browsed
by crows

fitful with with-
held flight

to break,

null bulk
buckling—we talk

as a dream
confesses itself, all at once
then slowly

into the ether
of the other and

out the
mouth, proud of its

speech

III

"The house suits me perfectly, the perfect
place for this not knowing where to be."

—César Vallejo

ATTACHED HOUSES

dim window

truckle un-

der the eye

wrinkled, slept-

in, gray linen

old woman

holding her-

self awake

like an o-

pen clothespin.

the window over-

looks—tare

in the rag-

weed, broom-

rape, catch-

fly, creeping fox-

tail—all

meticulous

twigs chewed to

sugar

residing in the

residuary

taking chaff not

wheat from what

on the threshing floor

was a durance

or thatch

whelmed by wind

with its soft metallic

integrity

dinted tin, bullet

nestled

in a thumb, age-

softened

delousing the chimes

and brooming out

the web

the typic rain

left the spider

bite of a mandolin

and one spider

dividend in

a water glass

as if held

in ludicrous tribute

then rubbed between

sooty palms—

sagging

catenaries, black

cutaways

blue, avid

black

jackdaws spade up

the sky, the wrong

yard

COAST

Overwatered

  grass

    rusts

Says

  I'll be lucky

    to die in this place

Sail's

  scalene leaning

    past wind-

    rippled pale tea

Leave the wavy

  transoms up

As a grief

  in being left

    rounds to a calm

STRAY

An adult escorted us back

from the drowning

we escaped

When the wiry boy

spit to the side

in the wind it hit

my face

We wanted to

know the undertow

existed

Stray waves collecting

behind the mind

into the shape of a hand

As promised

AIR AND DREAMS

latent, rain-
pungent, odd fondness to the fog
as it hugs her back

from him, the refrain of
a dream that
opens on

windowless inner
rooms

late talk   attains
a dim
saturation horizon
incision-line purple
ring of red wine
wide open

pretending to listen, she watches
air heal
a gash of smoke

her life lately
a charcoal figure
dusted down to contours

when pain states bare
its parentage

a gray grain lifting away

porch falls under
a perforated lid

twinkling alloy of
tin and twitchy
moth light

decay crazes
space, corners
everywhere, webs

sprinkled with gnats stuck fast
in cirrus prisons

once-white clematis
drawing in
sour air

pained, said
of her expression stretched

too tightly over
its frame

fabric first turbulent
then contented

by smoothing
shudders, what suddenness
pinched
shut

as a girl feeling
it flutter inside the net

air a loosely nerved
surface

falling over
a flying thing, so even

captivity
had loyalty   to dream

where body jaggedly
meets mind   define flight

a dream-
succession with puckered seams

on a dark walk   round-mouthed light of a silent note

anonymity
in balmy harmony

when the soprano   like a white napkin caught
on an iron weathervane
blows free

intimate chance

grace of a secret

                    hand-off,   of a secret's
deciduous
         and glancing
         hands

she stares into mismatched eyes
set shallowly in the ceiling

each unbares

abraded sky, gusty with birds

lights clinch in their gleaming arc
of *are*

air's arduous specks, spare
valuables

DIVINING

Now a white tricorne blowing over

        a lake, a fever not gold

but a snow-in-
summer – its surplus

       white tail and the havoc of our solder
hips holding
to
a *why*
shape. Ours was a runaway wooden

arm, stochastic
elm, finger-

wet—and our belly was a porous bed,
the felt rut of
a roman road, rivets

full of
sand. Now, in a flood, our buckets

escape us, the skulls
in the river rave

as if wood. What if we used the ears
to secure

the jaw? What if it grows too large

for a single heart?

FLOOD

If comfortable, compressible, then a liquid

state like waiting   —room silent with watery outline,

bricked-up hearth for a mouth

If silent, then invisible   —we start to whisper

when power goes out   —char on a white candle

from lighting others, smothering dark

in the solemn observance of storms

The room is warm though gaunt, like warning and the wait

that follows, oddly comfortable, compressible,

all give or interstitial distances, a field of feathers,

as they say, in a battle

of wills: The room, and rain raining now

through the ceiling   —water that has travelled

from an ocean into stone

coping on a shambling wall

MY BOUNDARIES

Love hovers

Grace halves

Anticipant steps

To the other

Room

To lose it

To loosen my unknowing borders

To loot the lying eye

I define my reaches generously

Traced antlers

Oafish mitt

With shallow sweet spot

Sweetly leaking to the grass

Wet-bottomed

Brown paper bag lifted like a rabbit

By the ears

NOTATION

Close storms, braille music.

Mud plucks the rain
like the gut

of a violin, warm in the palindrome
                    of arm
                    and chin—in-

tricate chit chat.
even as I write

          a rocking chair unfurls a choir of
          feral cats, and house

wrens, chiseled
maple, crackle

like real fire in the flue.

We too live in the neck of this hourglass,
in the downpour

of pause before the fickle
next note, the flicker in
a vein, a pulse

to feel in the figment, to feel for.

ACKNOWLEDGMENTS

Some of these poems, often in slightly different forms, first appeared in *Verse Daily, LVNG, jubilat, Seedings* (Duration Press), *Poem-a-Day* (Academy of American Poets), *Cincinnati Review, Propeller, Third Coast, Cake Train, elimae, Silenced Press*, and *Spoon River Poetry Review*.

Several of these poems were published in the chapbook *Attacked Houses* (Brooklyn Arts Press, 2013).

The book's opening epigraph, "Whatever you see, whatever can be taken away, is unspeakable" ("Lo que se ve, lo que se va, es indecible"), is from Alejandra Pizarnik's final uncollected poems, translated by Cole Heinowitz (published in *Jacket2*, February 2014).

Part I begins with an epigraph derived from the concluding lines of Gustaf Sobin's poem "Called It Space" in his collection *Towards the Blanched Alphabets* (1998).

The Tivka Frymer-Kensky quote that appears before "First Forty Days" is from her essay "Pollution in Biblical Israel," and I came to it via the book *The Purity Texts* (2006) by Hannah Harrington. The Joseph Ceravolo quote is from his short poem "Reborn" in his book *INRI* (1979).

The Cesár Vallejo quote that appears before "Attached Houses" is from "XXVII" in *Trilce* ("Esta casa me da entero bien, entero / lugar para este no saber dónde estar"), and the translation is a slight modification of Clayton Eshleman's translation.

ABOUT THE AUTHOR

Michelle Gil-Montero is a poet and translator of contemporary Latin American poetry, hybrid-genre work, and criticism. She has translated *Poetry After the Invention of América: Don't Light the Flower* by Andrés Ajens (Palgrave Macmillan, 2011); *Mouth of Hell* (Action Books, 2013), *The Tango Lyrics* (Quattro Books, 2013), *Dark Museum* (Action Books, 2015), *The Annunciation* (Action Books, 2019), and *Berlin Interlude* (Black Square Editions, coming in 2020) by María Negroni; as well as *This Blue Novel* (Action Books, 2016, National Translation Award semi-finalist) and *Edinburgh Notebook* (Action Books, coming in 2020) by Valerie Mejer Caso. She has been awarded fellowships from the NEA and Howard Foundation, as well as a Fulbright U.S. Scholar Grant to Argentina, a PEN/Heim Translation Prize, a SUR Translation Support Grant, and an Academy of American Poets University Prize. She is the author of the chapbook *Attached Houses* (Brooklyn Arts Press, 2013). She has an M.F.A. in Poetry from The University of Iowa and a B.A. in English from Brown University. She lives in Pittsburgh and is Associate Professor of English at Saint Vincent College, where she directs the Minor in Literary Translation. She is the publisher of Eulalia Books (eulaliabooks.com).

www.ingramcontent.com/pod-product-compliance
Lightning Source LLC
Chambersburg PA
CBHW031004090426
42737CB00008B/670